Helping Children Handle Stress

Other *Here's Life* books by H. Norman Wright:

Helping Teens Handle Stress
Crisis Counseling

A REASON FOR
Hope

Helping Children Handle Stress

H. Norman Wright

Here's Life Publishers

Published by
HERE'S LIFE PUBLISHERS, INC.
P. O. Box 1576
San Bernardino, CA 92402

HLP Product No. 951913
© 1987 H. Norman Wright
All rights reserved.
Printed in the United States of America.

Library of Congress Cataloging-in-Publication
    Wright, H. Norman.
        Helping children handle stress.

        (A Reason for hope)
        1. Stress in children.   2. Child rearing.   I. Title.
    II. Series.
    BF723.S75W76   1987   649'.124   87-8383
    ISBN 0-89840-190-9 (pbk.)

Unless otherwise indicated, Scripture quotations are from *The New American Standard Bible*, © The Lockman Foundation 1960, 1962, 1963, 1968, 1971, 1972, 1975, 1977.

For More Information, Write:

L.I.F.E. — P.O. Box A399, Sydney South, NSW, Australia
Campus Crusade for Christ of Canada — Box 300, Vancouver, B.C. V6C 2X3, Canada
Campus Crusade for Christ — Pearl Assurance House, 4 Temple Row, Birmingham B2 5HG, England
Lay Institute for Evangelism — P.O. Box 8786, Auckland 3, New Zealand
Great Commission Movement of Nigeria — P.O. Box 500, Jos, Plateau State, Nigeria, West Africa
Campus Crusade for Christ — P.O. Box 240, Colombo Ct. P.O., Singapore 9117
Campus Crusade for Christ International — Arrowhead Springs, San Bernardino, California 92414, U.S.A.

CONTENTS

Bitter are the tears of a child:
Sweeten them.
Deep are the thoughts of a child:
Quiet them.
Soft is the heart of a child:
Do not harden it.

Lady Pamela Windham Glenconner

1

THE WORLD OF A CHILD

Jimmy threw down his toy in frustration. This was the third time this week he had exploded. He was restless at school, and he was waking up two or three times a night. His mother couldn't understand why his behavior had changed so much. She was sure he was happy — after all, they were getting settled in their new home, and they finally had located a new church which would meet all their needs. This week they were even going to look for a new puppy to replace Jack, their collie which died three weeks before. Why was Jimmy like this?

You guessed it — stress.

Children experience stress a great deal more than we would like to believe they do. A child's world holds just as many problems for him as an adult's world holds for him. We may feel a child's stress is of less intensity or importance than that of an adult, but that is not necessarily true. Children's trials can be particularly traumatic for them, and can produce tragic long-term results. Troubled children need help in handling stress, and the sooner we can give them that help, the better chance they will have to grow and develop into emotionally healthy and mature individuals. In this book we are going to examine several aspects of stress in childhood and a number of things we can do to help our children cope with it.

Let's look right now at some of the sources of that stress. Can you remember what bothered you when you were in school? The fears, frustrations, uncertainties, pressures? Here, according to grade level, are some of the most common things that cause elementary schoolchildren to experience stress:

In *Kindergarten* the main stressors are uncertainty, fear of abandonment by an important adult, fear of wetting themselves, and fear of punishment or reprimand from their teacher.

First grade stressors are fear of riding the bus, fear of wetting in class, teacher disapproval, ridicule by peers, receiving the first report card, and fear of not passing to second grade.

In *second grade* the stressors include not understanding a certain lesson, fear of the teacher's discipline, fear of being different in some way from other children in class, and, often, missing a particular parent.

In *third grade* stress is felt from fear of being chosen last on any team or for any activity, having to stay after school, a parent-teacher conference, fear of peer disapproval, fear of not being liked by the teacher, fear of test taking, and not enough time to finish a test or assignment.

In *fourth grade* the stressors are fear of being chosen last for anything, fear of peer disapproval of dress or appearance, fear that their friends will find new friends and share their "secrets," fear of peer ridicule, and fear of not being liked by the teacher.

In *fifth grade* the stressors are just about the same as in fourth, but there is another concern as well, that of the possibility of not being promoted and thus not being a "big sixth-grader" the next year.

In *sixth grade* there are lingering and new stressors such as fear of being chosen last for anything, peer disapproval of appearance, feeling unpopular, fear of the unknown concerning developing sexuality, and fear of not passing to junior high — as well as fear of *going* to junior high.

These are just the stressors of school. When you add to this list all the things connected to the other parts of a child's life, you discover a multitude of potential stressors.[1]

What kind of things do you think would cause children to experience stress? Listed below are twenty situations that produce stress in a child. Which do you think are the most stressful? Pretend you are a child and rank these in order from 1 to 20 with 1 being the most stressful and 20 being the least.

CHILDREN AND STRESS

_____ Wetting pants in class
_____ Having an operation
_____ Giving a report in class
_____ Having a scary dream
_____ Being sent to the principal's office
_____ Going blind
_____ Moving to a new school
_____ Going to the dentist
_____ Being made fun of in class
_____ Acquiring a baby sibling
_____ Being suspected of lying
_____ Being held back a year in school
_____ Not getting 100 on a test
_____ Getting lost
_____ Receiving a bad report card
_____ Losing a game
_____ Hearing parents quarrel
_____ Being caught stealing
_____ Losing a parent
_____ Being picked last for a team[2]

Now compare your answers with those of the children in this study (which you will find near the end of this chapter). How close did you come? If you are like most parents, you will be surprised by the results. Does this exercise make you want to listen more closely to your children?

Why not ask your own children to rank these in the same way for themselves? You may be surprised.

Early Childhood — The "Magic Years"

Part of the process of understanding and helping a child handle stress is understanding how a child thinks and how he perceives life. Early childhood has been called the "magic years." The ages of three to six make up this time period. We call this the time of magical thinking because at this stage the child thinks he is omnipotent. He believes he is at the center of life and can affect what happens — he believes that his own thought process can influence objects and events in the world outside himself.

Because of this, he is unable to understand why his pet dies, or why he can't have what he wants when he wants it, or why he gets sick. He becomes quite disturbed with the unfamiliar bodily changes that accompany illness, and he often believes he causes the illness as well as other things that happen to him. Sometimes he feels he was bad or something is defective about him and that's why something bad happened.

He does not perceive life as unpredictable. We adults accept sudden events as just part of life. In fact, Scripture teaches us that life is uncertain and we should expect problems and upsets to occur, but a child has difficulty grasping this.

Because young children are egocentric (centered on themselves), they fail to consider the viewpoints of others. This has nothing to do with being conceited; it is just a normal part of the developmental process. They take things for granted and do not realize that other people need clarification. It's not until a child reaches the age of about seven that he begins to distinguish between his perspective and someone else's.

Three- to six-year-olds talk past one another. They have their own private speech and may not be talking to anyone in particular. They are not concerned whether you understand their words or not. They just assume their words have more meaning than is there.

A young child takes things at face value — literally. When a parent says, "I'm sick and tired of the way you are acting," what does a child think? He catches the parent's anger, but he also believes the parent actually may be getting both "sick" and "tired."

Think of the other phrases we say that are misunderstood. "Keep your shirt on"; "Hold your horses"; "That's cool"; and so on. Try to enter the child's mind. If you could hear what he is thinking, you would be amazed!

A child puts two and two together and does not necessarily come up with four for an answer. His connections are unique. Those connections make sense to him but to no one else. A child may see illness and going to the football game as related because his father became seriously ill the last time he went to the football game. A child may even become very anxious and avoid going to a game because of the connection he made.

When Brad was about six, he injured himself on the jungle gym at school, but he refused to tell his mother what had happened to him. After several days of questioning, all she could get him to say was, "I can't tell you." Over and over he would repeat this, sometimes even in tears. His mother was becoming increasingly alarmed over what really had happened to him until she began to make a connection. A friend of hers had died in a hospital just recently. Her son, she discovered, was afraid that if he told her what had happened, he would have to go to a hospital and — in his mind — if he did, he would die.

Middle Childhood

For children of all ages, stressors vary in their intensity. In the middle childhood years, different degrees of stress would be felt from such things as a poor grade on a test, the loss of a pet frog, rejection or ridicule by a friend, moving, and the separation or divorce of parents. And remember — children are more limited in their coping skills than adults. They don't have the repertoire of experiences to draw upon when faced with stressors and some of these things would be extremely difficult for a child to cope with.

Travel back in time with me and picture yourself as a seven-year-old child. You and your parents have just moved, and this is your first day at a new school in the middle of a semester. You didn't sleep well last night. Your stomach doesn't feel good, and you have to go to the bathroom a lot.

As you walk down the hall to your new classroom, you see other children looking at you. Some of them are giggling. You feel like turning around and running. You open the classroom door and thirty strange faces turn around and stare at you. Your heart rate increases and your stomach tightens up. The teacher makes you the focus of attention by telling the class that you are the new student, and then she proceeds to ask you your name. But the words just won't come out of your mouth! That is stress! Do you remember what it was like? If you do, you know that children need help.

Children from seven to twelve have changed considerably in their thinking. They have advanced in their ability to think conceptually. They are now able to work out some problems in their heads instead of just by trial and error. They can see the viewpoints of other people, and they recognize the feelings of others as well. Even their world of fantasy has changed. They now fantasize about real people and events instead of engaging in so much make believe. They can make sense of stress.

Children in the middle years are usually enjoyable

and uncomplicated, calm and educable. But they still have a difficult time dealing with anything that resembles intense stress. They prefer to avoid the issue and often will change the subject when you attempt to draw them into a discussion of their problems. They try to avoid the pain and anxiety. This is why many people who work with children of this age use games and play in the therapy process. Play allows children an outlet for what they are feeling and gives the counselor the information sought. Communication toys such as tape recorders, phones, drawing materials and puppets are very helpful.

However, even though these children have developed considerably in their thinking processes, they still tend to jump to conclusions without considering all the facts. Actually, children of this age group have a tendency to listen to contradictory information and not see the inconsistency. They often do not understand what they are hearing. Sometimes these children will not understand adults who are talking to them, and another real problem is that the adults often do not realize they are not being understood.

Following is the list of stress-producing situations in the order in which the original group of children perceived them, from most stressful to least stressful.

KID'S RESPONSES TO CHILDREN AND STRESS

1. Losing a parent
2. Going blind
3. Being held back a year in school
4. Wetting pants in school
5. Hearing parents quarrel
6. Being caught stealing
7. Being suspected of lying
8. Receiving a bad report card
9. Being sent to the principal's office
10. Having an operation
11. Getting lost
12. Being made fun of in class

13. Moving to a new school
14. Having a scary dream
15. Not getting 100 on a test
16. Being picked last for a team
17. Losing in a game
18. Going to the dentist
19. Giving a report in class
20. Acquiring a baby sibling[3]

We as parents cannot eliminate all the stresses of a child's life. Some of them will always be there. But we can do the following:

1. Realize that our children do live under constant stress.
2. Recognize any stressors that we or our environment tend to place on a child.
3. Take steps to eliminate those stressors which can be eliminated.
4. Teach our children how to handle the stressors of life.[4]

2

SOURCES AND SYMPTOMS OF STRESS

What is stress? Stress is any life situation that chronically bothers, irritates or upsets you. It is any type of action that places conflicting or heavy demands upon your body. What do these demands do? They simply upset the body's equilibrium.

Our bodies are equipped with a highly sophisticated defense system that helps us cope with those events in life which threaten and challenge us. When we feel pressure, we are infused with an abundance of adrenalin that prepares us for fight or flight.

If a child feels threatened, his body mobilizes its defenses, and the adrenalin disrupts his normal functioning and creates a heightened sense of arousal. He's like a rubber band that is being stretched. When the pressure is off, it returns to normal. When it is stretched too much, though, or kept in that wound-up position too long, the rubber band begins to lose its elastic qualities and to become brittle. It develops some cracks and eventually breaks. That happens to the child as well if there is too much stress in his life.

Stress has been called the wear and tear of life, the pressures of life, the "influential force." Some people think of it as tension and some as anxiety.

However, not all stress is bad. It is good when it gives us the pressure needed to stimulate us to action. Good stress, called "eustress," comes from the Latin word *eu,* meaning good. It motivates us, but it is positive and helpful because it does not last, nor is it experienced continuously. The body goes back to normal rest and recovery. When the body does not return to normal, we have bad stress, or *dis*tress.

Causes of Stress

The stress in a child's life can be caused when anything happens that

> — annoys him
> — threatens him
> — excites him
> — scares him
> — worries him
> — hurries him
> — frustrates him
> — angers him
> — challenges him
> — embarrasses him
> — reduces his self-esteem

Most of the time, though, it is not a particular event that causes stress. Whether we are children, teens or adults, most stress comes from our own minds. Damaging stress comes from threats that cannot be acted upon since they exist only in our imagination. Some children imagine the worst (and so do some adults). They worry, which creates more threat and imagined fears. Even when there *is* a definite threat to the body, the problem is in our mind. Situations that worry a child can be the most troublesome of all. On the other hand, a child who has learned to live according to "let not your heart be troubled, neither let it be afraid" (John 14:27) will be able to handle the pressures of life, both real and imagined, much better.

Other Contributors to Stress

In this booklet we will not be able to go into a lot of detail, but it is important to consider several other major contributors to stress: lack of proper rest and sleep, improper diet and the "hurry disease." Putting pressure on children to perform or to hurry wires their emotions and their bodies, and it makes relaxing difficult.

Think about a child's world. All day long children experience stimuli which can produce stress. The very state of change and flux they are in creates stress. And to top it off, they experience most of what adults experience: time pressure, high expectations, divorce in the family, illness, failure, violence, jealousy, etc.

Let's look at an adult stress study and apply it to the lives of children. The Holmes-Rahe Life Event Scale[1] serves as our example.

You will find below the forty-three life events listed in that scale. They have been adjusted to fit situations in the life of a child — that is, "spouse" is changed to "parent," "work" to "school," etc. The point value of each life event remains the same.

LIFE EVENTS

1. Death of a parent	100
2. Divorce of parents	73
3. Separation of parents	65
4. Parent's jail term	63
5. Death of a close family member (e.g., a grandparent)	63
6. Personal injury or illness	53
7. Parent's remarriage	50
8. Suspension or expulsion from school	47

9. Parents' reconciliation — 45
10. Long vacation (Christmas, summer, etc.) — 45
11. Parent's or sibling's sickness — 44
12. Mother's pregnancy — 40
13. Anxiety over sex — 39
14. Birth of new baby (or adoption) — 39
15. New school or new classroom or new teacher — 39
16. Money problems at home — 38
17. Death (or moving away) of close friend — 37
18. Change in studies — 36
19. More quarrels with parents — 36
20. (Not applicable to a child)
21. (Not applicable to a child)
22. Change in school responsibilities — 29
23. Sibling going away to school — 29
24. Family arguments with grandparents — 29
25. Winning a school or community award — 28
26. Mother going to work or stopping work — 26
27. School beginning or ending — 26
28. Family's living standard changing — 25
29. Change in personal habits (e.g., bedtime, homework, etc.) — 24
30. Trouble with parents — lack of communication, hostility, etc. — 23
31. Change in school hours, schedule or courses — 20
32. Family's moving — 20
33. A new school — 20
34. A new sport, hobby or family recreation activity — 19
35. Change in church activities — more involvement or less — 19
36. Change in social activities — new friends, loss of old ones, peer pressures — 18
37. (Not applicable to a child)
38. Change in sleeping habits — staying up later, giving up nap, etc. — 16
39. Change in number of family get-togethers — 15
40. Change in eating habits — going on or off diet, new way of family cooking — 15

41. Vacation   13
42. Christmas   12
43. Breaking home, school or community rules   11

Totaling the score, you may be surprised to find how quickly an average child can reach the 300-point level of severe stress potential. Changes occur rapidly in a child's life, far more rapidly than in the life of his parents. Six hours of school alone can subject him to the possibility of any combination of life events 8, 10, 15, 18, 22, 25, 27, 31, 41, or 43 on almost a routine basis. In addition, the ups and downs of his social life add the chance of stress from life events 13, 17, 32, 36, 39, or 41. He is especially susceptible to personal injury because of the high percentage of his time spent in physical activities such as bike riding or skating. In addition, he may fall victim to any contagious disease that strikes the school.

Symptoms of Stress in Your Child

You may be asking, "How do I know if my child is under a lot of stress?"

There are many symptoms. If these symptoms occur frequently and persistently, listen to the message that's being given to you.

Some of the symptoms are:

- chronic irritability
- difficulty concentrating
- difficulty sleeping or difficulty staying awake
- poor eating habits such as impulsive, uncontrolled eating
- restlessness
- rapid heart rate
- backaches
- neckaches
- headaches
- muscles aching for no apparent reason
- irritating behavior

— lack of spontaneity ("He's just not himself lately.")

— frequent mood shifts

— nervous habits such as twitches, nail biting, pulling at hair, biting lips

If you notice these signs, especially a combination of them, you can be fairly sure that your child needs help to learn to respond to life in a new, healthier manner.

Identifying Sources of Your Child's Stress

Whenever you observe the symptoms of stress in your child, you should attempt to identify the source. Look for its beginnings. You may want to ask yourself some of the following questions:

1. What is the source of this stress? Is it within the family (such as Dad taking a new job which requires frequent absences)? Or is it outside the family (failing a major math test)?
2. Does the stress affect all the family members (such as a death), or just the child (having a close friend move away)?
3. Was this stressful experience sudden (accident) or did it come on gradually (observing a close friend get sick and then die)?
4. What is the degree of the stress? Is it intense (a death of someone close) or mild (a cold which causes the child to miss a soccer game)?
5. Does this stressor require a short-term adjustment (starting a new school) or is it long-term (mononucleosis)?
6. Was the situation expected (knowing a close friend is moving) or was it unexpected and unpredictable (a fire in the home)?
7. Do the family members feel the stressor is one which can be adjusted to (going to a new school) or is it beyond anyone's control (father lost his job and has no prospects in sight)?

Continue to be aware of every stressful situation. Each one carries with it both pain and the potential for growth.

Teaching Your Child to Spot Stress

The potential for stress is all around us. The problem lies in how much of it a child experiences and how long it lasts.

It's important to teach your child how to recognize stress when it occurs. This can be done best by helping the child recognize the symptoms. If your child came to you and asked "What is stress? How do I know when I have it?" what would you say? How would you describe stress to a child?

Perhaps you could say, "Stress can result from what happens between people. Your friend may be mad at you, or the students in class may have made fun of you and it really hurt. It can occur when you don't get enough sleep or when there is too much going on. In addition, you can cause your own stress by what you think about yourself. If you think you're dumb or no good or not pretty, those ideas can cause stress."

In explaining what stress is to your child, you may want to use the "Have you ever . . . ?" approach:

Have you ever had your heart beat faster?

Have you ever had your hands get cold and sweaty?

Have you ever had your stomach get in a knot?

Have you ever had your tummy hurt?

Have you ever gotten nervous?

Have you ever felt sad or giggled a lot?

Have you ever felt mean, or like crying, or that you wanted to get back at someone?

Have you ever had frightening dreams?

Have you ever not been able to concentrate?

Have you ever been grouchy?

Have you ever not gotten along with others?

(And any others you can think of.)

If a child understands that these symptoms could be caused by stress, it can help him to monitor his own life and use some of the stress reduction suggestions given later in this book.

Childhood is a long time of life, a time of preparation, growth and development. During this period, children face some of the same stressors as adults, but without the same resources. You can help your child by explaining what stress is and how to recognize it when it occurs. Help him monitor his life.

3

A CHILD'S FEARS

One way to understand the stressors of children is to understand their fears. Why? Because so much of childhood stress stems from fear.

How do we recognize a child's fears? What are the indications that anxiety is present? Some children are very verbal about their fears and you have little difficulty being aware. Others either avoid thinking about them or make it a point not to share them. However, whether he talks about it openly or not, if a child is fearful or troubled with anxiety, you probably will notice some of the following symptoms.

Symptoms of Fear

Children who have difficulty concentrating and who become either listless or hyper may be struggling with inner anxiety. They could be experiencing stress. If their appetite changes from eating very little to consuming greater amounts of food, this too could be a sign of anxiety. Bedwetting, nightmares, restlessness, insomnia, unusual talkativeness, stuttering, panic attacks, compulsive behaviors or obsessive thought patterns are additional indications of fear. Often a wide range of bodily complaints will be the indication of fear or may accompany many of the above.

One grandmother said to me, "I can always tell how my daughter and son-in-law are getting along by how much my granddaughter is stuttering."

Some Specific Basic Fears

Let's look at some of the basic fears of childhood as suggested by Erik Erikson (who has pioneered studies in the developmental stages of life).

Children fear withdrawal of support. This pressure can be felt both at home and at school, and children fear the withdrawal of peers as well as that of adults. Being too smart or not smart enough can turn peers away. Wearing the wrong clothes can have the same affect!

QUESTIONS (to ask your child): What kind of help do you like? How do you feel when someone takes it away? How can you handle this?

Children fear suddenness. Infants respond to sudden movements around them with a startled response. This continues throughout childhood. Adults may plan deliberately for some time to make major moves such as taking a new job and moving into a new home in another state, but for the child, it doesn't become a reality until it happens. This is true even if it has been discussed with him before. He needs much talk and anticipatory planning.

QUESTIONS: What kind of sudden, unexpected things frighten you the most? How can we learn to handle these?

Fear of noise takes its toll on children, even infants, and we live in a noisy world. Four-month-old Lee became visibly agitated when his mother set a wound-up music box down beside him and turned it on. She had to take it away.

QUESTIONS: What noises bother you the most?
How can you learn to handle noise?

Fear of interruption can be a real frustration to a child. A child's concentration on an activity can be intense, but an adult often will interrupt since, from the adult's perspective, that activity isn't important. However, playing, reading, talking, watching TV, or even just sitting around — any of these can be extremely meaningful activities for a child.

QUESTIONS: What interruptions bother you the most? How can you handle the interruptions that can't be avoided?

Children fear having something important to them taken away. If you are a parent, you already know how possessive children feel toward "their" things. These can be tangible things such as a rock collection, or they can be something intangible such as being the best student in the class. The child fears losing either.

QUESTIONS: What are you most afraid of losing?
How can you handle losing something?

You know that children are afraid of too much restraint, but do you know they also fear too much freedom? Children do not like to be tied down by too many rules or restrictions, but an overabundance of freedom gives them more independence than they can handle. A balance is needed between restrictive parents and schools and permissive schools and parents.

QUESTIONS: What kinds of restrictions or rules bother you the most? What are the times you wish there were more rules or restrictions? What can you do when there are too many or not enough rules? How can you learn to handle this?

Children fear being exposed. In school there is one

question that many children dread hearing, the one that comes when a test paper has been returned and the child has seen his bad grade — his friend turns around and asks, "What did you get?" Children feel exposed when they try for the honor roll and don't make it. Some children experience exposure when their parents listen in on their private conversations on the phone — these children learn to be secretive.

QUESTIONS: How do you feel when someone finds out something about you that you don't want them to know? What could you say or do to handle that time better?

Strange as it seems, many children fear being small or remaining small. One of the status symbols in our society is bigness. Big houses, big athletes, big babies — all are given notice. In school, older students appear so large to a child that his own shortness is magnified. Boys are concerned about the size of their penis and girls want to be the first in their group to wear a bra. What does a child feel when others call him or her "Shorty"?

QUESTIONS: How do you feel about your size? What size do you want to become? What will you do if you end up smaller than that?

A fear common to both adults and children is being left alone. Girls, especially, feel this fear, which accounts for the strong cliques formed among preteen girls.

Separation from mother is one of a child's greatest fears. Unfortunately, we live in a society where children are separated from their parents a great deal — because of divorce, both parents working, too many outside activities, pressures at home, or neglect. In school, children are upset when a favorite teacher leaves or when they are punished by being isolated from the rest of the class.

QUESTIONS: How do you feel when you are left alone? When might you be afraid of being alone? What does it feel like when you are lonely? What can you do to handle the lonely times?

More Fears

In addition to those listed above by Erik Erickson, here are two more common childhood fears, along with some suggestions as to what can be done about them.

For many children an *animal* is an object of fear. (It is for many adults as well.) How do you help a child who is afraid of an animal? One thing you *don't* do is force the child to face the fear all at once, for he does not have the resources to cope with it.

Let's assume that a child is afraid of cats. A cat may appear small to us but look at it from the child's point of view. A thirty-pound child looking at a fifteen-pound cat sees something different from what you and I see. If you can imagine a cat that is half or a third of your weight, your response might be a bit more cautious. Also, even though cats look harmless, their claws are sharp. They sometimes bite, and they are unpredictable. How do you then help a child? (The following approach can be used with many other animals or fear objects as well.)

Instead of pushing the child toward his total fear, try gradual exposure. Show him pictures of a cat or point out the qualities of cats on the various ads on television. Let the child watch you demonstrate your joy in handling a cat. Let the child know that he can pet the cat as you do. Don't force him to do so, but when he does touch the cat, talk about how soft the cat's fur is, how pretty it is, etc. It is important to select a cat that is calm and one that responds positively to love and attention. Encourage the child to pet the cat with you more and more frequently. The time will come when the child is able to do this on his own and be spontaneous about it.

Some parents have found it helpful to have the child keep a written record of his progress regarding whatever it is that he fears or that upsets his life. Such a written record shows the child he is attaining a goal. For example, the record might indicate when the child responded to a cat, how long, where, and what his positive feelings were.

In addition to the fear of animals, *nighttime fears* — such as fear of the dark and of nightmares — are very common.

Darkness can be especially frightening to a child, for it generates a sense of feeling isolated, abandoned or lost. A gradual approach once again can be helpful. A child needs to know that it is all right to talk about his fears, that he will not be made fun of for being afraid. You might try gradually reducing the amount of light in the child's room. Share the following verse with the child and help him commit it to memory:

> When you lie down you shall not be afraid; yes, you shall lie down and your sleep shall be sweet. Be not afraid of sudden terror and panic, nor of the stormy blast or the storm and ruin of the wicked when it comes [for you will be guiltless], for the Lord shall be your confidence, firm and strong, and shall keep your foot from being caught [in a trap or hidden danger]" (Proverbs 3:24-26, *The Amplified Bible*).

Many children have nightmares or, as they call them, "bad dreams," three to six times a month. When you or I take a fear to bed with us it often crops up again in our dreams — our minds run wild during our sleep. So we realize that children's persistent and repetitive nightmares may indicate that excessive tension, stress or fear has been felt during their day. When their dreams occur nightly or several times a night, consider that it may be telling you something. (For specific and detailed help with children's fears see *Helping the Fearful Child* by Dr. Jonathan Kellerman, W.W. Norton and Company.)

To understand your child's fears and anxieties better, ask him what he thinks about when he is going to sleep at night. Ask him if he's ever afraid or if he ever worries. Read him the following poem and see how he responds.

WHATIF

Last night, while I lay thinking here,
Some Whatifs crawled inside my ear
And pranced and partied all night long
And sang their same old Whatif song:
Whatif I'm dumb in school?
Whatif they've closed the swimming pool?
Whatif I get beat up?
Whatif there's poison in my cup?
Whatif I flunk that test?
Whatif green hair grows on my chest?
Whatif nobody likes me?
Whatif a bolt of lightning strikes me?
Whatif I don't grow taller?
Whatif my head starts getting smaller?
Whatif the wind tears up my kite?
Whatif they start a war?
Whatif my parents get divorced?
Whatif the bus is late?
Whatif my teeth don't grow in straight?
Whatif I tear my pants?
Whatif I never learn to dance?
Everything seems swell, and then
The nighttime Whatifs strike again!

Source unknown.

You might want to share with your child some of the worries you can remember having when you were young as a way to encourage your child to share his with you. You could make a game of it. Read a list of your own "whatifs" to your child and then ask your child what his "whatifs" are.

How We Can Help

Children learn most of their fears. This means that it is also possible for them to unlearn them. Dr. Kellerman suggests a number of practical and workable ways to help children rid their lives of fear:

1. Let the child know that *it is all right to be afraid.* Everyone has fears at some time in his life. A certain amount of fear is normal and we don't have to be ashamed when we are afraid. Share your own childhood fears and let the child know that those fears passed from your life. This can be an encouragement to him.

2. Help the child understand that *being afraid is temporary.* He may even fear that his fear will last forever. Children need a message of hope for the future.

3. Let the child know that *it is good to talk about his fear.* Sharing it helps him keep it in perspective and avoid distortions. His sharing will help you to know the extent of his fear, and then you are better equipped to help him overcome any distortions. Many parents have found it easier for the child when they have him draw his feelings or fears on a piece of paper with crayons, or act out his fantasies, or use puppets to talk out his fears.

4. Let the child know that *it is also normal not to be afraid.* When a child can observe another person not being afraid in a situation where he is fearful, he gets the message that it is possible not to be afraid.

5. Help the child learn that *a new behavior will replace his fear response.* These new responses are called counter behaviors or fear-replacing behaviors. Encourage the child to imagine himself not being afraid in his usual fear experience. These kinds of positive imageries are powerful substitutes which we could all use to greater effectiveness. Even encouraging a child to become angry in his fear situation can be beneficial. It is difficult to be both fearful and angry at the same time. The anger will give him a greater feeling of control. Participating in a positive activity or favorite pastime when the feared object or situation is at hand can eventually lessen the fear.

As with adults, so with children — repeated facing

of a fear is the best method of overcoming it. We all need to use the creative powers of our God-given imagination to visualize ourselves handling the fearful event. Depending upon the comprehension level of the child, selected portions of Scripture will help bring peace and comfort to his mind.

One of the underlying themes of fear for both children and adults is the fear of the unknown. We desire certainty. We want to be assured that we will be all right, that we will be safe, that our questions will be answered, and that we will be able to do what we are asked to do.

Many of our other specific fears have their roots in this fear. However, though we may not know all that will happen, God does know. The psalmist says, "Thou knowest my downsitting and mine uprising, thou understandest my thought afar off" (Psalm 139:2, King James Version). One of the great lessons of life for a child is to come to the place where he can say, "It's all right for me not to know all the answers because I trust in God and He helps me handle life's uncertainties."

Let me talk with you now about what may be one of *your* fears as a parent. You may be apprehensive about recognizing the fears in your children's lives. Don't be too hard on yourself. Most of us received little or no training in how to be a parent before our children were born. And even if we had, our humanity would still show through. We are not all-knowing and there are no guarantees in parenting. God does expect us to do our best, but He doesn't expect us to be perfect. (I would encourage every parent to read the outstanding book by Marilyn McGinnis, *Parenting Without Guilt,* published by Here's Life Publishers.)

4

DEPRESSION IN CHILDREN

Perhaps it seems odd to discuss depression in children as a problem, but depression is not a respecter of persons.

A child's depression often goes undetected by the adults around him. This condition in children is probably hidden more successfully than when it occurs in any other age group. The child doesn't realize he is depressed, and even if parents suspect something is wrong, they often deny their child is chronically unhappy. They fail to recognize, accept or respond appropriately to the child's symptoms. After all, who wants to admit his child is depressed?

Recognizing the Symptoms

How do you recognize childhood depression? Here is a composite picture of how a child would appear if every characteristic of depression were included.

First of all, the child would appear quite unhappy. He would not verbally complain of this, and he might not even be aware of it, but his behavior would give you that impression.

This sad child also would demonstrate withdrawal and inhibition. His interest in normal activities would diminish. He would appear listless, and his parents would think he is bored or sick. Often concerned parents begin looking for some symptoms of a hidden physical illness, and indeed there could be some physical symptoms that further blur the earmarks of depression. These symptoms include headaches, stomachaches and sleeping or eating disturbances.

Discontent is a common mood. The child would give the impression of being dissatisfied. He would derive little pleasure from what he does. People often wonder if someone else is responsible for the way the child feels.

The child would feel rejected and unloved. He would tend to withdraw from anything that might be a disappointment to him. As with other age groups, a negative self-concept and even feelings of worthlessness would be present.

Irritability and a low frustration tolerance would be seen, but the child would be unaware of why he is upset.

Sometimes, however, he would act just the opposite, attempting to deal with his depressive feelings by clowning around and provoking others. He especially may act this way at a time of achievement because he would find it difficult to handle something positive. This provocative behavior makes other people angry.

Now of course, these characteristics will not all be present in every case of a depressed child. When several of them are obvious, though, or any one is particularly intense, depression should be suspected.

Sometimes children experience and express their depression in the same way as adults, but not always. However, enlightened adults can recognize the symptoms fairly easily. Because of their limited experience and physiology, children tend to express their depression as rebellion, negativity, anger and resentment. The depression expressed when parents divorce, for example, may be manifested by bedwetting, attacking friends or siblings, clinging to parents, failure in school or exaggerated story-telling.

Differences Due to Child's Age

The signs and symptoms of depression vary with the child's age. Even infants can be depressed, and an infant who is depressed simply may not thrive. Generally speaking, children age two to five are less apt to experience depression than those younger or older. However, a parent's moods may severely affect a small child. For example, a mother who is depressed may withdraw from her child, who in turn also becomes depressed. The problem is that the child usually cannot overcome his depression until the mother overcomes hers.

Looking for the Causes

Why do children become depressed? It could be caused by any of the following: a physical defect or illness; malfunction of the endocrine glands; lack of affection, which can create insecurity in the child; lack of positive feedback or encouragement for accomplishments; death of a parent; divorce, separation, or desertion by a parent; parental favor toward a sibling; poor relationship between the child and a step-parent; economic problems in the home; moving to a new home or school; punishment by others.[1]

Look for any type of loss that may have occurred in the child's life. This could be the loss of a pet or friend, a severe rejection experience, a divorce situation, or a death in the family. A child's thoughts and feelings due to the loss of a parent through divorce probably will be similar to and as intense as those experienced when there is a death. Whatever the type of loss, try to see it from the child's point of view. It is easy to misinterpret a child's perspective, especially if you have not been around children very much.

Help for the Younger Child

Depression in the younger child is a normal reaction to a perceived loss, and you as the adult need to accept it as such, whatever the cause may be. Allow the child a period of time to adjust to the loss. Let your child know that everyone experiences sadness and depression at one time or another. But be sure to put it into terminology the child can understand. Explain that feelings like this are normal and that in time they will go away and the child will feel better. Encourage him to tell God about his feelings and assure him that God understands our down times as well as our happy times.

As a child goes through the adjustment process, keep in mind the characteristics of both the magic years of the younger child and the middle years of the older child. A child in either age group will need to:

— accept the pain of the loss;
— remember and review his relationship with the loved person;
— become familiar with all the different feelings that are part of grief — anger, sadness and despair;
— express his sorrow, anger and sense of loss to others;
— verbalize any feelings of guilt;
— find a network of caretakers. He needs many people to support him at this time.[2]

The younger child especially will need to be helped to experience the depression as fully as possible. Resisting or ignoring the depression merely prolongs the experience. Encourage the child to be as honest as possible in expressing his feelings, in admitting that he is depressed or sad, and listen without being judgmental or critical. He needs your support.

If grief is involved, you need to allow the child to

do the grieving naturally. If the grief is over divorce, do not expect the child to get over it quickly. This type can last a long time and it can recur from time to time.

Help the child find some type of activity that will bolster him. A new game, a sight-seeing trip, or anything that would interest him may be helpful.

Find a way for the child to experience some type of success. Remember what he has done fairly well, and help him use that special ability again. His self-esteem can be rediscovered and elevated through small successes.

Help the child break out of his routine. Even such simple items as a new food at a meal or taking him to a special restaurant may help. Taking a day off for an outing may be particularly helpful.

Help for the Older Child

What can you say to your older child who is going through depression? For openers, you can say simply, "I care for you and am available. I want to be with you." Put your arm around your child and hold his or her hand. There is healing in the physical touch. A pat on the back, or holding the arm will convey acceptance. Be honest and tell your child, "I don't understand all you are going through, but I am trying — and I'm here to help you."

Most parents don't know what to do for their depressed child. Here are some practical guidelines. How closely you follow these will depend upon the intensity and duration of your child's depression. If it is for only a few hours or a day or two, or if the child is feeling down but is still functioning, not all of the suggestions would apply. But if the depression has lasted for quite a while, and the child is dragging around, not functioning, not eating or sleeping, you should apply the appropriate measures.

1. *Understand the causes and symptoms of depression.* If your child is so depressed that he just stares, ignores

greetings, or turns away from you, remember that he doesn't want to act that way. In depression, the person loses the ability to govern his thinking and his emotions. If he is severely depressed, he cannot control himself any more than you could walk a straight line after twirling yourself around in a tight circle twenty-five times. Understanding the normal behavior of a depressed child will enable you to control your own responses better and you will be able to help your child more effectively.

2. *Watch out for the possibility of suicide, even with children.* Unfortunately, this tragic problem is on the increase. The family of any depressed person should be aware of the potential of suicide. Any individual who is so depressed that he talks about a hopeless future might be considering ending his own life. Every hint or allusion to suicide should be talked about. Ask the child to tell you about his suicidal thoughts or plans. It will help him if the subject can be brought out into the open. Then he knows that other people are aware and can be called upon for help and support.

3. *Get the depressed child to a doctor* if the condition continues. Your family physician may be able to help, or he may recommend someone who can. The time factor is very important. Don't let depression go on and on.

   As long as you tolerate a child's depression, you help maintain it.

4. *Give the child your full support* but don't overreact. The entire family needs to be made aware of the situation and instructed as to their responses. Strong discipline with a depressed child should be suspended until he achieves greater stability. Ask the family not to attack the child, not to bring up his failures, not to come down hard on him, and not to ask him to do things he is not capable of doing while he is depressed.

5. *Don't avoid the depressed child.* He doesn't have the plague. Avoidance further isolates him and could

make him feel worse. You might be avoiding him because you feel guilty about his depression, thinking
you are the cause. Remember that one person may
contribute to another's problem from time to time,
but no one person is responsible for another person's
happiness.

6. *Understand that a depressed child really hurts* and it
may be worse for him since it's hard for him to understand why he feels so bad. Don't suggest that he
does not feel bad or that he is just trying to get your
sympathy. Don't tell him to "snap out of it." Don't
tell him that all he has to do is "just pray to God
about it," giving him the impression that that will
solve everything.

7. *Empathize, rather than sympathize, with your child.*
Sympathy only reinforces a child's feelings of hopeless-
ness. It may make him feel more helpless and may
lower his already low self-esteem. Statements such
as "It's so awful that you are depressed" or "You
must feel miserable" or "How could this ever happen?"
rarely help.

8. *Make sure the child eats.* If he doesn't want to eat,
you can say, "Look, you may not feel like eating, but
you probably are hungry. Starving won't help. Food
is important, so let's eat now. I'll sit down and eat
with you. And then let's talk about what's troubling
you." Don't harp on the food problem, though, or
on his eating habits. Saying "You'll make me feel bad
if you don't eat this food" or "Think of all the starving
people" won't get him to eat. Instead, it will probably
make him feel worse. Remember, not eating is a
symptom of being depressed.

9. *Keep the child busy.* Physical activity during severe
depression can be more beneficial than mental activity.
You might need to schedule the child's entire day for
him, and all preparations should be made in detail.

If your child loses interest in activities he normally
enjoys, you can remind him gently of the fun he had

before with those activities, and then firmly and positively insist that he become involved. Don't ask him if he would like to, because he might not know, or he may not care to respond. Don't get angry and say, "You're going with me because I'm sick and tired of you sitting around feeling sorry for yourself." Rather, you could say, "I know that you haven't been feeling well, but you are entitled to some enjoyment. I think you might like this once we get started. And I would like to do this with you."

Perhaps you could phone to find out what time a school activity begins. Upon hanging up you say to your child, "I think we can get ready for it, so let's start now." If you are going shopping, you could suggest, "Come along. I like to have someone with me. You're good company and I need your advice."

Any activity such as a social event, or calling a friend to play can be used. By getting involved, the child begins to break the destructive behavior patterns, and this helps him gain energy and motivation.

10. *Don't ever tease your child or lecture him about his lack of confidence.* But don't ignore it either. Loss of confidence and self-esteem is common in depression, and it must be faced. In reactivating self-esteem, help the person see the illogic of his self disparagement. Don't join in his self pity. Rather, look for past accomplishments and get him to focus on what he was able to do before he began to feel so bad. You can say, "Perhaps you can't do some things the way you did before, but let's talk about the things you still do well. What do you think they are?"

If he says, "I can't do anything," gently name something he can do, or try to draw it out of him. At this point you are trying to help him overcome his sense of helplessness.

Be persistent and steady in your responses to the child's depression. Remember that at this point you have more control over your emotional responses than he has over his.

If the depression is severe and the child does not respond, he should have professional help. However, there are many depressive childhood experiences a parent can handle without taking the child for counseling. By following these principles, you will be much more able to fulfill the biblical teaching on giving empathy and encouragement, and you will be guiding your child toward a considerably more positive attitude toward life.

> Bear one another's burdens, and thus fulfill the law of Christ (Galatians 6:2).
> Therefore encourage one another, and build up one another, just as you also are doing (1 Thessalonians 5:11).

5

THE STRESS
OF DIVORCE

One of the most stressful things that happen to children is the divorce of their parents. That can be nearly the most traumatic experience a child will ever have to face.

Newsweek magazine has estimated that 45 percent of all children will live with only one parent at some time before they are eighteen. Twelve million children now under the age of eighteen have parents who are divorced.

The effects of divorce on children have been shown to be more serious and longer lasting than many divorced parents are willing to admit. Studies released in England in 1978 showed that children of divorce have a shorter life expectancy and more illness than those in families where no divorce occurred. These children leave school earlier as well. In New York City, which has a very high adolescent suicide rate, two of every three teenage suicides involve teenagers whose parents are divorced. Many other teens carry a pattern of insecurity, depression, anxiety, and anger into their adult years.[1] On the average it takes a child up to five years to adjust to the impact of his parents' divorce.[2]

What a Child Loses

In divorce, children experience many losses. These can include not only the loss of one of the parents, but also the loss of home, neighborhood, school friends, family standard of living, family outings, family holiday get-togethers, and so on.

A child's self-esteem is put in serious jeopardy, too. Have you ever wondered what it would be like to learn, as a child, that your parents are divorcing, feel the panic of it, and then have to face telling your friends? Fear becomes a daily companion, and the losses multiply.

When a child loses a parent, he also may lose his hope for the future. Because of the uncertainty, a child can feel out of control to a greater extent than ever before. The parents upon whom he depended are no longer the solid rock he needs, and the shakiness of his situation can soon show up in such areas as family finances. If a divorced father has promised to take care of the family and his monthly payments become irregular, and then eventually cease, the child's uncertainty becomes more acute — and what emotional loss must he feel regarding his father's apparent lack of concern for him? This is an additional stressor.

How Age Affects Reactions

Divorce affects children in different ways depending upon the age of the child.

Young children of *three to five,* and even younger, become fearful; the routine separations of life become traumatic. A parent's going shopping or the child's leaving for preschool is a stressful experience.

These children tend to regress to earlier behavior patterns and become more passive and dependent. More

and more they ask questions like What's that? in an effort
to overcome the disorganization of the crisis. They have
a great need for affection. They may refuse to feed themselves, and some even revert to a need for diapers. They
can create wild and imaginative fantasies in their minds
because they are puzzled by what is happening to them.
They are bewildered. Play does not have the same sense
of fun. These preschoolers may become aggressive with
other children.

In addition, some psychologists believe that the ab-
sence of a parent of the opposite sex could be damaging
to the child's sexual development.

When you are counseling a three- to five-year-old
child whose parents are divorcing, help the child verbalize
his hurt and his idea of why his parents are divorcing.
Throughout all the stages of childhood, a common thought
is *Did I cause my parent's divorce? Am I responsible for
not having a family any more?* As we mentioned before,
a child this young has unrealistic perceptions and may
feel as though his behavior or thoughts actually caused
the divorce. It is not easy to convince him otherwise, but
it is vital to try to help him to see other possibilities.

The *six- to eight-year-old* child has his own set of
reactions. Sadness is there, and his sense of responsibility
for the parents' breakup is stronger. His feelings of loss
are deep. He is afraid of being abandoned, and sometimes
even of starving. He yearns for the parent who has left.

Frequently these children are angry with the parent
who cares for them all the time. They have conflicting
loyalties. They want to love both parents, but they struggle
with the feeling that loving one is being disloyal to the
other. Thus they feel torn and confused. Symptoms can
include nail biting, bedwetting, loss of sleep, and retreat-
ing into fantasy to solve family problems. Children of
both age groups become possessive.

Preadolescent children of *nine to twelve* usually experience anger as their main emotional reaction. This anger is felt toward the one the child feels is responsible for the family breakup, who could be the custodial parent. However, instead of leveling his anger directly at the parent, he may aim it at his peers, alienating them at the time he needs them most.

The child of this age also suffers from a badly shaken self-image. Some of these children will throw themselves into what they are doing with great intensity as their way of combatting that and of handling the disruption of their lives.

A Child's Two Main Concerns

In all the turmoil of divorce, children seem to have two major concerns.

The first is their dream that their parents will reconcile. The children believe that if this were to happen, all their problems would be over. They think that, in spite of previous problems, the family was better off when both parents were there. The child may have seen the conflict, but he is usually willing to tolerate the conflict in order to have an intact family. After all, this is the only family he knows.

His second concern revolves around himself — what will happen to him? He is afraid that the parent he is living with will abandon him. One parent already did. Why shouldn't the other?

If one parent was forced to leave (as many are), the child's fear centers on being thrown out as his mother or father was. Again, this is a stressor.

Another fear concerns being replaced in the parents' affection by someone else. As the custodial parent begins to date, the child wonders if this new person is going to become important to his parent. And if so, he fears he may lose the time and attention he now receives.

Helping the Child Through His Emotional Reactions

In order to help the child of a divorced couple, it is important to understand what he experiences. Remember that his feelings will change with the passage of time. There are fairly clear emotional stages through which a child passes as he struggles to understand and deal with a divorce. These stages are normal, and they cannot be avoided or bypassed. They have nothing to do with the spirituality of the child. Your goal, in endeavoring to help the child, is to guide him as he passes through these stages in order to produce positive growth and minimize the negative effects.

Shock. Although a child's home may be filled with visible conflict, the child rarely expects his parents to get a divorce. He may not like the conflict but hopes it will settle down eventually. Discovering that a separation or divorce is going to happen is usually a great shock to a child.

Fear and anxiety. These unsettling emotions occur because the child is now faced with an unknown future. In the past a home and family with two parents has been the child's source of stability. It is now about to be shattered.

Fear and anxiety may manifest themselves in restlessness, nightmares, sleeplessness, stomach problems, sweating, and aches and pains. These are normal problems. A child needs to be given reassurance. It is important to give him the facts, because a child's imagination may run wild, and knowing is better than wondering. A child may tend to think up worse problems than actually exist.

Feeling abandoned and rejected. After fear and anxiety come feelings of abondonment and rejection. The feelings of the initial stage recede and are replaced by this struggle. The child may know at one level that he will not be rejected or abandoned, but at a deeper level he is still concerned that it might happen. A younger child has difficulty distinguishing between the parents leaving one another and their leaving him, and he may focus on this. This stage of the child's emotions may be perpetuated by unkept promises on the part of the parent who leaves.

Loneliness and sadness. Feeling sad and alone soon replaces the sense of abandonment and rejection. As the family structure changes and calms down, the reality of what has occurred begins to settle in. A child feels this stage with a pain in the stomach and a tightness in the chest. This is the time depression begins, and regular activities tend to be neglected. Many children do a lot of thinking, which is usually wishful daydreaming. These fantasies follow the same theme — parents getting together again and everything being all right. Crying spells may become more frequent at this time.

Frustration and anger. These feelings are the next to come — children whose parents divorce or separate become angry children. This is a natural response to the frustrations they feel. In addition, they have seen upset and angry parents, and the children emulate this modeling of anger. The anger may continue to be the pattern for many years and, unless dealt with and resolved, probably will carry over into many adult relationships.

The child's anger is there for several reasons. It serves as a protection and a warning signal, just like depression. It is often a reaction to hurt, fear or frustration, and it alerts others to the fact that there is a problem.

The anger may not show itself directly. It's an inward, basic feeling which, rather than being expressed openly, may be suppressed or masked. It may become evident, then, through a negative perspective on life, or through irritability, or withdrawal and self-isolation. Anger also may be expressed through strong resistance — to school or chores, or whatever the child wants to resist.

Anger is an involuntary response, so don't be threatened by it or attempt to deny its presence in the child. Rather, help the child learn to express and drain it. According to his ability, help him to understand the cause for his anger, and its purpose. If it is not allowed a direct expression, it can come out in an indirect manner, and may erupt in violence. This exhibition would indicate displaced anger and is far more dangerous than allowing a child to acknowledge his anger and speak openly about it.

Resentment and rejection (on the part of the child). Eventually the child's anger moves to resentment and resulting rejection by the child. He is not over his angry feelings but is now attempting to create some emotional distance between himself and his parent. This is a protective device. Pouting can be one of his forms of rejection, as can the silent treatment. The child won't respond to suggestions or commands, and he often "forgets" to follow through with what he is supposed to do. He becomes hypercritical as well.

This behavior is actually a reaction formation. As a child pushes a parent away, he really wants to be close to the parent. He makes hateful statements and yet wants to be loving. He is trying to protect himself from being rejected, so he rejects first.

Reestablishing trust. The final stage in the child's problem of dealing with parental divorce is the reestablishment of trust. It is difficult to say how long this will take, as it varies with each situation and child, and can range from months to years.

What can parents or adults do to help? Here are some suggestions:

1. Do not be so concerned with your own feelings that you neglect the child's feelings. Give him some time each day to discuss what he is experiencing and feeling.
2. Allow the child time to process his feelings. There are no quick solutions or cures.
3. A stable environment is beneficial to the child. It's better for a child not to have to move but to live with his remaining parent in the same home and neighborhood with as many things as possible staying the same. Of course, some change will be necessary, and the

child will need to adapt, but the parent must realize that the greater the change, the greater the stress and discomfort to the child.

4. Give positive feedback to the child, and build his sense of self-confidence.

5. Reassure him that he is not the cause of the divorce or separation. Both parents need to give him consistent and equal amounts of love.

6. According to the child's level of understanding, help him to know in advance the different types of feelings he will be experiencing. Keep the child informed at all times of any environmental changes expected so he can be prepared.

A child needs to be assured that even though his mother and father will be working through their own struggles as the divorce proceeds, they still will be taking care of him. Parents, friends, and other relatives need to repeat this to the child often so he begins to realize that more than one person is supporting him with this belief. This is an especially appropriate time to assist the child in selecting some interesting task that he can accomplish to help overcome his feelings of helplessness, of being out of control.[3]

6

HELPING CHILDREN COPE

For adults and children alike, stressors are a part of daily life and we don't worry too much about most of them. When a child breaks a finger, we assume he will recover. When a child has chicken pox, we wait for him to get well. When a child has a cold, we know he will get over it.

When a child has an ulcer, however, or excessive fatigue, or a psychosomatic illness, that's a different matter. It's not so easy to deal with these conditions — which are caused by stress.

One way to identify the child who is having difficulty with stress is by using The Capable Kid Test. It also will help you assess your child's stress level and you will be better prepared to show him how to cope more effectively.

THE CAPABLE KID TEST

Step 1. Think of a situation that your child has experienced as stressful. It could be sharing a room with a sibling, having a favorite weekend outing canceled, flunking a test, not making the school team or play, being shunned by friends, being embarrassed, etc.

Step 2. Think about how he reacted and whether that is his typical response to that type of situation.

Step 3. Choose *one* statement from the following list that best describes his reactions. (Select the first one that strikes you as accurate.)

1. "Things like this always happen to me."
2. He becomes unreasonably quiet and walks away.
3. "I never get what I want. Nobody cares about me." (May become belligerent and verbally abusive.)
4. "Boy, am I disappointed" (then a few seconds later, "Oh, well, maybe it will work out next time").
5. "This is no surprise. I was expecting something cruddy like this to happen" (then becomes withdrawn and preoccupied).
6. "That sure makes me angry. But I didn't know. Is there anything I can do now about it?"
7. "That is just not fair. It's not fair" (and proceeds to have a temper tantrum).
8. Doesn't visibly react, but just withdraws. Won't talk about it and tends to isolate himself.

Step 4. Now, find the description of your child as indicated below. Remember, the description you have selected should be your child's typical way of responding.

#4 or #6 — This is a capable child. He handles stress well. This person will express disappointment or anger and then quickly figure out what to do about it. He will be disappointed rather than upset, but it will last only a few minutes.

#1, #2, or #7 — This child is slightly vulnerable. He has upset reactions, but they don't last very long. He soon calms down, becomes less preoccupied with himself, and begins to make statements about how he can handle the problem. He could learn some new ways of coping so he wouldn't be so reactive.

#3, #5, or #8 — This is a seriously vulnerable child. His response usually lasts more than twenty-four hours, and symptoms of being vulnerable are evident in his life. [1]

Here are some of the most important characteristics of the capable child and the vulnerable child:

The Capable Child
 — resourceful
 — confident
 — able to confront people or situations when concerned or upset about something
 — willing to take risks
 — relaxed
 — responsible
 — able to express feelings easily
 — endowed with a sense of direction

The Vulnerable Child
 — withdrawn, preoccupied
 — often sick without an organic cause
 — isolated
 — secretive, noncommunicative
 — belligerent, uncooperative
 — overly sensitive
 — in need of excessive reassurance

How We All Cope

How do children approach life's stressors? Basically, they follow the same pattern we adults follow. There are four main ways in which we all try to cope:

1. We attempt to remove the stressor.
2. We decide to refuse to allow neutral situations to become stressors.
3. We try to deal directly with the stressor.
4. We look for ways of relaxing to ease the tension of the stress.

Both adults and children use these methods every day. Let's look a little more closely at each method.

Can a child remove a stressor? Occasionally, but usually he doesn't have the necessary power or control. In fact, children often are stuck — with no hope of removal — in a situation which becomes a source of intense stress, so they deal with it by inventing means of getting out of its way. A child may give up her friends because their behavior is either contrary to her standards or frightening to her — or both. Or, during a family fight she may go to her room and turn up her radio to drown out the noise.

As for neutral situations in a child's life, they sometimes get turned into stressors by other people. Exams at school are a case in point. They can be the source of acceptance or rejection by significant adults such as the child's teachers or parents. Some children worry about the exam whereas other children refuse to let it pressure them by making statements to themselves like, "Why shouldn't I get a fairly good grade? I've studied and I've done all right so far. And even if I don't, it isn't the end of the world. I'm still OK."

What about confronting a stressor head-on and dealing directly with it? That may take figuring out a way to get around it. A child who is tired of being kidded about being heavy can go on a diet and lose weight. I saw a child in a class go up to a teacher and ask to have his seat moved because he talked too much to his friend who sat next to him, and he was tired of getting into trouble for it.

What about relaxation? How can children find a way to ease the tension when stress is facing them? How do *you* relax? Do you take breaks, jog, play tennis, run, read a novel? These hobbies and activities which are engaged in for enjoyment are a source of relaxation for us. Have you taken your child to the public library and introduced him to the wealth of material found on the shelves?

Learning to read novels at an early age provides one source of relaxation for him. You can help him find others. Unfortunately, we often structure our children's activities so strictly that they have little time just to be a child. After-school sports are often overly competitive with an emphasis upon winning instead of on the enjoyment of the activity. We tend to be result oriented rather than to do things just for the joy of it, and we project that philosophy onto our children. However, the child needs a model in relaxation from us. Tim Hansel's book *When I Relax I Feel Guilty* will assist you in helping your child find some necessary ways to relax.

Many children feel just what this little poem reflects:

> I wish I was a rock a-settin' on a hill;
> I wasn't doin' nothin' but just a-settin' still.
> I wouldn't eat, I wouldn't sleep,
> I wouldn't even wash.
> Just set there for a thousand years or so
> And rest myself, by gosh!
>
> Source unknown.

To consider further those four ways of handling stress, answer each of the first four questions below in reference to your child. Then ask your child to answer the next list of questions.

1. How do you see your child removing stressors in his or her life?
2. How do you see your child refusing to allow neutral situations to become stressors?
3. How do you see your child dealing directly with stressors?
4. How do you see your child relaxing?

Now ask your child:

1. How do you handle upsets and frustrations?
2. How do you refuse to let some problems upset you?

3. How do you handle a problem head-on?
4. What's the best way for you to relax?

(You may have to change the wording of some of these, depending upon the age of your child.)

Helping Children Learn

How can we help our children learn to handle the stressors of our age more successfully?

One of the best descriptions I have heard of helping young children is that it is like working on a jigsaw puzzle. You ask them to discover the pieces, you point some of the pieces out, and you help them fit the pieces together.

Here are some practical things you can observe as you attempt to help your child cope with the disappointments and stress in his life.

As an adult, you need to use the child's language and be flexible in your communication. You must actively guide your conversation with a young child or you will end up failing to communicate. In working with your child, you need to make your statements very clear and even rephrase them several times. Repeat and repeat patiently. What may be clear to you simply may not register with your child.

Young children have one-track minds. They often focus on one aspect of an event to the exclusion of all the others. They cannot see the forest for the trees. If you throw too much information and too many events at a child in one conversation, he cannot handle them. You need to introduce other aspects of the situation gradually as he is ready to take them on. Your task will be to help the child see all the aspects, to organize his thoughts, and to explore other possible reasons for the stressful situation.

Whenever you try to help a young child, remember these facts: The child feels responsible for what has happened to initiate the stress; he makes connections different from the ones you make; he is egocentric; he has unrealistic and immature perceptions.

If this is how children think, what can you as a parent or teacher do to help this child who is under stress? Sometimes it will be impossible to fully change the child's pattern of thinking. You need to accept this as a fact of life and lessen your own frustration. Helping a child fully express his inner thoughts and feelings is one of the best approaches. This helps him gain greater self-control in a crisis event. By expressing his thoughts aloud, he can move to a new position. Patiently repeat your questions to the child, and encourage him to think aloud. Help him uncover the most probable or real reason for what is occurring. Try to help him discover this himself instead of giving him the reason. Look for any indications of guilt that the child may be experiencing.

A child needs time alone with his parent each week. This can be difficult if there are several children in the family, but it is needed. Parents need to be good listeners and help their child express his feelings, which in turn will help resolve his anger and frustrations.

One of the best ways a child learns to handle stress is through observation within the home whether the family consists of both parents, one parent and a dog, grandparents, or those in a foster home. The positive attitude and modeling of the important adults in a child's life will give the child a firm foundation for dealing with the stresses of his life. (Since I am assuming that you are an adult reading this booklet, let me suggest two resources for your own reading: *Less Stress* by Dave and Jan Congo ((Regal)) and *How to Have a Creative Crisis* by myself ((Word)). In this latter book, see the chapter on the questions of life.)

Children Who Cope

Children who are able to cope with the stressors of life accept their strengths and their limitations. They are also individualistic. They respond to peers, and they have a number of friends, but they still maintain their own individual identity. In contrast, peer-oriented children are less sure of themselves and have a lower opinion of themselves. Because peer pressure becomes so vital and influential during the adolescent years, it is important for preadolescent children to be aware of and able to maintain their own identity.

Children who cope are able to express their feelings to others. They can share their hopes, anger, hurts, frustrations and joys. They don't bottle up their feelings.[2]

If your child struggles with this, sit down with him, listen to his feelings of disappointment, and work with him on the alternatives. You may want to come up with a few suggestions including the ridiculous as well as the serious.

When one eight-year-old boy wanted to do something, and was disappointed and upset because he couldn't, his mother told him, "I know five different ways you can handle this disappointment, John, and some of them may work. If you want to hear them, let me know." In ten minutes he was back, asking what they were.

"You really want to know?" his mother said.

John grumbled and said, "Yes."

"Well," she said, "here they are. Maybe some are all right and maybe some aren't." She sat down with him and shared the following:

1. "I could go to my room and throw my clothes out the window to show everyone I'm upset."
2. "I could write a letter to God telling Him how disappointed I am and then read it to a friend."
3. "I could call eleven of my friends and complain to each of them."
4. "I could set the timer on a clock and cry for forty minutes until the bell rings."
5. "I could tell my mom that I'm disappointed and then we could talk about what we could do instead and

maybe plan for this activity another time."

This mother and son ended up with a very interesting discussion.

Like some adults, some children are not overly affected by the stressors of life. Why? Who are the children who seem to handle the stressors of life best? They all seem to have some of the same characteristics. They can concentrate instead of jumping around from one thing to another. They can handle frustration. They can work at a job until it is finished. They have learned to accept the disappointments of life, or they find alternatives. They also are able to postpone gratification. This is an important key. The children who handle stress well are those who can wait.

In addition to what we have discussed before, helping a child understand, commit to memory, and apply significant passages from the Word of God to his life is probably the most effective solution to stress.

A few of the passages which can become a source of stability and comfort to a child are:

James 1:2,3
Philippians 4:6-9
Psalm 37:1-9
1 Peter 5:7
Isaiah 41:10,13
Psalm 27:1
Isaiah 26:3
Psalm 4:8
Hebrews 13:6

Read these verses yourself. Then write out how you would explain the meaning of each verse to a child. How would you help the child apply the passage to his own situation?

The child will learn best by seeing the reality of these passages lived out in the life of another individual. He needs to see the powerful effect of Scripture, and he needs to see that it does make a difference when a person puts into practice what God's Word has to say.

NOTES

Chapter 1

1. Dr. Bettie B. Youngs, *Stress In Children* (New York: Avon Books, 1985), pp. 55-57. Adapted.
2. Donald C. Meadows, Barbara J. Porter and I. David Welch, *Children Under Stress* (Englewood Cliffs, NJ: Prentice-Hall, 1983), pp. 10-12.
3. Ibid., pp. 11-12.
4. Mary Susan Miller, *Childstress* (Garden City, NY: Doubleday & Co., Inc., 1982), pp. 26-33. Adapted.

Chapter 2

1. Mary Susan Miller, *Childstress* (Garden City, NY: Doubleday & Co., Inc., 1982), pp. 22-23.

Chapter 4

1. Brent Q. Hofen and Brenda Peterson, *The Crisis Intervention Handbook* (Englewood Cliffs, NJ: Prentice-Hall, 1982), pp. 21-39. Adapted.
2. E. Lindemann, "Symptometology and Management of Acute Grief," *American Journal of Psychiatry* (1981), 139:141-48.

Chapter 5

1. Archibald Hart, *Children and Divorce: What to Expect and How to Help* (Waco, TX: Word Publishers, 1982), pp. 124-25. Adapted.
2. *Marriage and Divorce Today* (May 18, 1987), 12:42, n.p.
3. H. Norman Wright, *Crisis Counseling* (San Bernardino, CA: Here's Life Publishers, 1986), pp. 167, 172. Adapted.

Chapter 6

1. Antionette Saunders and Bonnie Remsberg, *The Stress-Proof Child* (New York: New American Library, 1984), pp. 31-32. Adapted.
2. Mary Susan Miller, *Childstress* (Garden City, NY: Doubleday & Co., Inc., 1982), pp. 42-53. Adapted.

More Help For The Tough Times.

WHEN YOUR CHILD IS ON DRUGS OR ALCOHOL. Professional counselor Andre Bustanoby shows how to help your child make responsible choices and how to help your child face up to his/her destructive behavior. 951368/$2.95

HELPING TEENS HANDLE STRESS. Marriage and family expert H. Norman Wright addresses one of today's most pressing issues: the stress today's teen encounters through peer pressure, school, and the search for identity. A must for parents and youth workers. 951764/$2.95

HELPING CHILDREN HANDLE STRESS. H. Norman Wright shows how instilling healthy patterns of stress management in young children will help produce a better-adjusted, confident and responsible teenager. A must for parents and children's workers. 951913/$2.95

WHEN YOU'VE BEEN ABUSED. Professional counselor Andre Bustanoby offers practical help for those who have lived with the nightmare of incest or mental/physical/verbal abuse. 951384/$2.95

WHEN YOU HAVE FAILED. If you're discouraged by a recent failure in your life, Andre Bustanoby will show you how to use the situation as a stepping stone to great accomplishment. 951350/$2.95

WHEN YOU'VE BEEN WRONGED. Professional counselors Frank Minirth and Paul Meier offer effective strategies to help you overcome the hurt and bitterness of being wronged by another person. *Available August 1988.* 952077/$2.95